From Prison to Power

Your Prison Starts In Your Mind

Kent Osbourne

Contents

"This real life story From Prison To Power will be a blessing to the multitudes. It will encourage, empower, & inspire people from all walks of life."

- Carlton McConnell(CEO) Round The Clock Entertainment

"When you mention the word inspiration, Kent Osbourne has to be considered as one of the best inspirational speakers of the year and years to come. He's faith lead, headstrong and has extreme determination that propels him. He is inspiring others along the way that you can be young, successful and strong mentally just as much as physically. I will say he definitely inspires me to get up and get out to make something out of my life. Thanks Kent Osbourne."

- Lil L

"Kent Osbourne it has certainly been an encouragement to sit back and watch you soar. In this life our Heavenly Father challenges us. Your pain from the past has built an awesome man of god full of passion and love. I admire you and believe in you as we may have lived different lifestyles. You have been a motivation to me spiritually as I'm rebuilding myself since I have not always appreciated where I am. I'm so proud of you."

- MM

"Kent Osbourne is a very inspirational out going young man. He has the utmost respect and love for people and God. Kent has a never die attitude in which he is very determined to accomplish and complete any goals that he sets. He is the founder of Prison To Power nonprofit organization in which he mentors young people encouraging them to realize they can be successful with determination and a little hard work. Mr. Osbourne is definitely an inspiration to me. Bless you in all your endeavors."

- Kenneth Davis (Uncle Kenny)

"Kent Osbourne goes hard at whatever he sets his goals to. Through his encouraging messages, he makes you realize that you can be successful despite the odds against you with hard work, ethics and determination. He has dedicated his life to inspire the youth. It is his love for God and people that motivates him to keep encouraging and inspiring others. May the Lord bless and keep you in all that you do."

- Renee' Dianne Davis (Auntie)

Dedication

In loving memory of my mother Willia Jean Osbourne who is no longer with us and my father Kent Alysious Osbourne who is also no longer with us. Although you are not here I want to thank you for bringing me on this earth and staying with me for the short time you did, which was the best days of my life. I thank you for instilling Christ into me. I will never understand the reason God took you both so early, but God doesn't make mistakes.

Through your passing I have had multiple challenges and setbacks that the average person probably wouldn't have been able to bounce back from. I do believe everything that I have been through was for this purpose. To help motivate, inspire and save lives which I have been anointed to do. I've turned my pain into passion and I'm going to help save the world.

I'm proud to say I'm the son of two great parents Willia Jean Osbourne and Kent Alysious Osbourne that left this earth too soon. I love you mom and dad. I know your looking down from heaven smiling on me. To my most favorite people in the world Willia Jean Osbourne, and Kent Alysious Osbourne, I would like to dedicate this book to you.

Author's Note

I lost my dad when I was 5 in Wood Hall, Jamaica. He got very ill and passed away. I was very sad. I couldn't believe my dad was gone. I felt like I was being cheated out of life. I had lost my best friend. My dad and I were close. He would take me to work with him to the orange grove and I would enjoy working beside him learning entrepreneurship skills. He had his own business as a fruit contractor. Experiencing death for the first time in my life wasn't an easy task. Seeing my dad laying up in that glass that covered his casket was devasting. I really loved my dad.

By me having a strong mom that stepped up in place of my father made the process of being fatherless a lot easier to deal with. Knowing I had a praying mother who believed in God helped me to make it with my father being gone. My fathers death brought my family closer as we knew that someone you loved could be snatched away from you in a blink of an eye and that we had to make every second of us being together priceless. My mom was very strong. She was torn to have lost a good husband who was a provider, hard worker and great father. She remarried a few years after my father passed.

My mom gave birth to three sons. Ricky, Kenneth and Kent Osbourne. Kenneth and I were the sons of my dad Kent Alysious Osbourne Sr. My brother Ricky who was the oldest had a different dad from Kenneth and I. Ricky's dad was American. After facing all kinds of trials and tribulations, roadblocks, stumbling blocks and everything life threw at me that was set up for me to fail, I survived. Not only have I survived, I made it and I want to help motivate and inspire others that may be going through some of the same things as me in this book. Maybe you have a love one that may be going through it. They can make it. Whatever situation they are in at this moment it is not over, there is still hope. God has been blessing me tremendously and now it's time for me to give back and be a blessing to others. This is my story "From Prison To Power".

Chapter 1

Loud Knock At the Door

I heard a loud knock at the door four in the morning that woke me out my sleep. My step dad, who was tall, fat and black with big yellow teeth with gaps in them got up to answer the door. I got out of bed and walked to my bedroom door that was already opened to see who was knocking on the door that early in the morning. My step dad asked, "Who Is it"? It's the Madison County Sherriff Department, said the man at the door. My step dad opened the door. There stood two tall white males in their mid 30's with brown eyes and blond hair. Both men had sheriff badges pinned to their sheriff's suits with shiny black shoes. "Is everything okay officer", asked my stepdad. "May we come in", one officer said. "Yes", my step dad said as he opened the door all the way up and stepped to the side to let them in.

"There's been a terrible car accident in which your wife was killed, your daughter is in a coma", said one of the sheriff's. "Lord No", cried my stepdad as his knees got weak and he fell to the ground. Tears began to roll down my face. By that time my brothers had awaken and heard the bad news. We all sat in the living room comforting each other as we stayed up crying the rest of the morning. The next day my brothers and I was taken to my grandmother's house which wasn't too far from where we lived.

We stayed there a couple nights because we didn't want to live with my stepdad who we never got along with. My aunt Rosetta pulled up to our grandmothers house and knocked on the door. My brother Ricky opened the door to answer her. My aunt Rosetta walked inside. She was a tall brown skinned woman with jet black hair and bifocals on that made her eyes big and scary. "Gather up all ya'll things and take them to the car", she said.

We did as we were told as she went into the other room to speak with my grandmother. My brothers and I went back into our grandmother's house after putting our things in the car to give our grandmother A final kiss, hug and good bye. After saying our final goodbyes, we got into aunt Rosetta's car and we headed back to Melbourne, FL where we grew up and where most of our family lived.

What did you learn? How will you implement?

_____

_____

_____

_____

_____

_____

_____

_____

_____

_____

_____

_____

_____

_____

_____

_____

_____

_____

_____

_____

_____

_____

_____

_____

_____

_____

_____

_____

_____

_____

_____

_____

_____

_____

_____

_____

_____

_____

_____

_____

_____

_____

_____

_____

_____

_____

_____

_____

_____

_____

Chapter 2

Runaway

My brothers and I arrived back in Melbourne, FL to my aunt's house a few days after my mom passed on a Friday. We pulled into the driveway to a white and orange four-bedroom house with a car porch. I remembered the house from visiting her in the past. "We're here", says aunt Rosetta. "Gather your things out the car and take them into the house and I'll show you to your rooms", she said. We did as we were told and was shown to our rooms. Monday morning, we got up and had to register for school. I was registered into Meadowlane Elementary school. After arriving back home after school Aunt Rosetta loaded us up into the car.

"Come on boys we're going shopping for ya'll some clothes", says aunt Rosetta. After a short ride we pulled up to an old run down white building with older folks walking in and out. We got out and walked in. There were clothes lying on tables and some on hangers. Everything in the building had been worn by other owners in the past and brought there for resale. "Ok boys find you some clothes that you like", said aunt Rosetta after asking us our sizes. My older brother and I looked at each other and did as told. We weren't happy with the fact we were shopping for used clothes.

As I got older I started to play all kinds of sports. I played baseball at a park called Lipscomb Park, basketball at Grant Street Community Center and football at Brothers Park. Out of all the sports I played I became an Allstar player at football. I was the best on my team. I played running back on offense and fullback on defense. I never came off the field because I was that good. Every year I played I made Allstar. I played for the Redskins which was the name of our city league football team. My aunt never came to support me with nothing. I didn't see the love and she didn't give me the drive. I had to do it all on my own.

In school I was a straight A student, very smart and intelligent. I was the morning announcer at my middle school. Every class had TV's in them. I was the one on TV every morning with the school morning announcements. I excelled in school. Even though I was so smart and intelligent, on the inside I still was hurt and bothered. There still was something missing in the inside that caused me to act out in school. One day I participated with locking our teacher in the closet in our shop class.

He would be scared to enter the closet. He had to go back and forth into the closet to get material for us. When he would go in one of us would sneak up, close door and lock him in. He would scream, "open this dang door"! Sometimes he wouldn't get out until the next class arrived. I would get into fights in school but never get caught a lot of times. I was very sneaky. I would participate with my friends fighting against skin heads, which was the white people with the shave heads who we felt was prejudice.

Back at home my aunt would get mad at us and start to curse, but never finished the word. She would say things like, "boy I'll beat you're a__, but never would add the ss, until she started saying it so much until the whole word would come out sometimes. My aunt was a Christian woman that was saved by the grace of God even though she wasn't perfect. She kept us in church. Every Sunday and sometimes through the week we were in church. We would be in church so long that we would sneak out church and walk home. My younger brother was a chunky little fellow and he use to hate for me to call him juicy. That word would make him so angry that he would act out and fight me. All I had to do was move my lips like I was saying it and he would act out. I would call him juicy when we would be next to my aunt and get him in trouble.

Sometimes I would just move my lips. My aunt would whoop us and I really hated that and felt we were being abused because it wasn't my mom whooping us. I thought she was doing it because she hated us. There was a talent show at my elementary school. I wanted to be in it, but I couldn't let aunt Rosetta know, because if she found out I was dancing to Hip hop I would have been in some deep trouble. So, my aunt Rosetta's daughter helped me out big time. I put together a singing group which consisted of my younger brother, my cousin which was aunt Rosetta's daughter son, and my cousin friend.

I loved Another Bad Creation at that time. Another Bad Creation was a boy group out of Atlanta, GA. I orchestrated the whole thing to dance like them and we won the talent show. After winning that talent show I was so excited! I knew being an entertainer was something I had a passion for and wanted to do for the rest of my life. It was amazing to be in front of a crowd doing what I loved to do.

I was very nervous performing in front of people for the first time, but I pulled it off! Aunt Rosetta's daughter took us and brought us back. Aunt Rosetta never knew what happened.

One day my aunt and I got into a big argument when I was 14 years of age and I couldn't take it anymore. I yelled out, "I don't want to live here anymore, this house not big enough for me"!

Well how big do you want it to be, yelled aunt Rosetta!

"I miss my momma, I want my momma back", I screamed!

"Well your momma never coming back"! She's gone, aunt Rosetta screamed back!

I ran to my room and slammed the door. Later that night around midnight I packed all the clothes I could and jumped out my room window and ran for dear life to my cousin Jesse house.

What did you learn? How will you implement?

_____

_____

_____

_____

_____

_____

_____

_____

_____

_____

_____

_____

_____

_____

_____

_____

_____

_____

_____

_____

_____

_____

_____

Chapter 3

Jesse House

I ran to my cousin Jesse house. My cousin Jesse was a short heavy set red skinned woman with short black hair. My cousin Jesse was one of the coolest cousins I had. She was like an aunt and I loved staying the night at her house as a kid. I knocked on the door and Jesse came to the door yawning dressed in an all-white night gown with some slippers on and cold still in her eyes and halfway asleep. "Boy what you doing up this time of night?" She asked. "Hey Jesse can I live with you?" I asked her. I don't want to live with aunt Rosetta no more she's too mean!" I said. "Well what does aunt Rosetta think about that?", said Jesse. "I don't care what she thinks I can't take it anymore."

"All the fussing and whooping me and she not even my mom." "I jumped out the window when she was asleep and came over here." "I'm not going back over there Jesse", I told her with that look in my eyes that I was serious, that even if God himself came down he wouldn't be able to get me to go back over there. "Well let me talk to aunt Rosetta tomorrow and see would she turn you over to me, "Jesse said. The next day Jesse talked to aunt Rosetta and aunt Rosetta agreed to turn custody over to her and the money aunt Rosetta was getting for me for my parents being deceased.

Jesse worked a lot which gave me a lot more freedom than a normal 14-year-old to do what I wanted to do, plus she didn't care to much what I did as long as I took my behind to school. Jesse had a brother named Corn. Corn was a big heavyset light skinned guy that was a true hustler. The only thing in life Corn knew how to do was sell drugs. Corn had dropped out of school to pursue a life of crime selling drugs. I wanted to be just like him after seeing the money, cars, jewelry and all the beautiful women he slept with. I would watch him and learn things about drugs. One day I was walking with bags of weed on me which I was trying to sell in a school zone. Officer Simpson rolled up on me in the school zones.

Officer Simpson was a tall black neighborhood cop that stood about 7 feet tall with a deep voice, low haircut and always liked to wear shades. "Hey boy come here", yelled officer Simpson. When I saw he was coming I dropped the drugs to the side and stepped on them. "What up Simp", I said. "Empty your pockets boy", said Simpson. "For what?" I yelled back. Officer Simpson walked up to me and started to search me.

He searched one side of my pockets, then the other and didn't find anything. Then he told me to step to the side, he was aware that I had did something with the drugs. When he then moved me to the side and seen the drugs I was stepping on I took off running. As I was running away I could hear officer Simpson saying, I know where you live boy.

The next day officer Simpson was at my cousin Jesse house looking for me. He told my cousin Jesse what I had did and he took me to the police station where I was released back to the custody of Jesse. See Simpson had remembered me from when I had stolen my cousin car from my aunt Rosetta house not that long ago and he had come to my school to scare me up.

As the days went by I met a friend in school and his name was D. We had become good friends and I got to know his mom and dad. I would go and spend the night at his house without asking Jesse. Until Jesse yelled at me about not asking her and for not telling her where I was. Then I started asking her for permission to go places. One day we went to this girl house that D was dating. We had to sneak through her bedroom window while her mom and dad was asleep. The deal D had made with me was when we get inside, he's going to get in the bed with her and have sex with her and as soon as he gets off he wanted me to climb in the bed with her.

So, once we got inside the window he got in the bed and I got on the floor. I could hear the bed moving and her moaning as he slid inside her. Once he was finished having sex with her, he told her that I wanted to have sex with her to and talked her into it some kind of way. She seemed uncomfortably with it and went back and forth with him about it, but then she agreed because of D. Then he waved his hands for me to come up and I did. He got off the bed. Then I took off my clothes and put on the condom that my friend Derrick gave me and showed me what to use to keep girls from getting pregnant and me catching diseases. I put myself inside of her. I had never felt this feeling before. I was only 14. It was a warm wet feeling As I stroked I could feel something rising and erupting like a volcano. Then all of a sudden, BOOM!

I could feel myself being drained. I pulled out and jumped off the bed, took off the condom, and Derrick and I hopped back out the window. We jumped on our bikes and headed back to Derricks house.

What did you learn? How will you implement?

_____

_____

_____

_____

_____

_____

_____

_____

_____

_____

_____

_____

_____

_____

_____

_____

_____

_____

_____

_____

_____

Chapter 4

Caught In the House

A year had then went pass. I was 15 now. I had started dating this girl name Steph and I really loved her, at least I thought I did. I was too young to know what love was. Steph was a white, slim girl with brown eyes, brownish straight long hair, tall and very pretty. My friend Gem was dating her friend. So, we got on our bikes and headed out to Palm Bay from Melbourne where we lived. My girl had told me her parents were gone for the weekend and left them there alone. So, when we got there we hid our bikes and knocked on the door. Steph answered the door and let us in.

My friend Greg and I stayed the night over and enjoyed the festivities and all the sex these girls were giving us. Then on this particular day while we were in Steph room, her parents came home unexpectedly! Scared as I don't know what we had to figure something out! So, Steph told us to jump in the closet and we did. Her parents came in the house and I could hear them talking but couldn't make out what they were saying.

Then all of a sudden, I hear Steph room door open and her dad ask, "Who do you have in here?" "No one", said Steph. Then her dad walked around the room. He looked under the bed and didn't see no one. In the closet my heart was racing and was about to jump out my skin. Gem was scared to. Then her dad turns toward the closet and opens it. Bam! We were busted! "What are ya'll doing in my house?", he yelled!

"I'm sorry sir I just was over visiting Steph", I replied. "Well you could have just asked me instead of sneaking in", he said. "Yes sir, it won't happen again", I said. I was so scared I didn't know what to do! He lectured us. Steph was in deep trouble. "Now get out my house", he screamed! Gem and I ran out the house, got our bikes and took off down the road.

What did you learn? How will you implement?

_____

_____

_____

_____

_____

_____

_____

_____

_____

_____

_____

_____

_____

_____

_____

_____

_____

_____

_____

_____

_____

Chapter 5

Boxing

I was starting to get into a lot of trouble at my cousin Jesse house because she worked so much and was never there. Jesse was best friends with a cousin of mine that introduced me to her little brother Trey which was also my cousin. Now Trey was a little taller and older than me with a muscular frame, low haircut and one gold teeth in his mouth. Trey was a boxer who boxed for the P.A.L. which stood for "Police Athletic League", which was intended to keep kids off the street and out of trouble.

Jesse registered me with P.A.L. Trey and I began to hang together and become the best of family. Trey was very good at boxing and was well known around the city for boxing. Trey wasn't the saint everyone thought he was. I would smoke weed with some of my friends and hide it from Trey, because as a boxer we weren't supposed to smoke. I was very talented in boxing which led me to being called K.O. by my cousin Trey. Even though my initials were always K.O.

I was never called that until I started boxing. I had this boxing match in Palm Bay, Fl against a man who was older than I was. As the first round started we started to box. As he threw punches I was throwing them back. I was very good at using my left jab as my lead to set the opponent up for the right hand. I kept sticking and moving. This guy was a brawler. As we exchanged punches I caught him with a hard right to the nose and he fell to the floor.

The ref pushed me back and gave him an eight count and he got up. As we started to box again I kept hitting him with the left jab and blood started to leak from his nose and unto my gloves. The ref would stop the fight to wipe the blood. As we continued to box we would start to brawl and I would get a little winded and my mouth piece would fall out. As we continued to box I knocked my opponent down three times but I was later disqualified for dropping my mouth piece.

I wasn't doing it intentionally, I just wasn't use to it being that this was my beginning stages being in the ring. As the months rolled by I got better and better and started to win more fights but eventually ended up quitting boxing to live a life of crime where I felt I would be more successful.

What did you learn? How will you implement?

_____

_____

_____

_____

_____

_____

_____

_____

_____

_____

_____

_____

_____

_____

_____

_____

_____

_____

_____

_____

_____

_____

_____

_____

_____

_____

_____

_____

_____

_____

_____

_____

_____

_____

_____

_____

_____

_____

_____

_____

_____

_____

_____

_____

_____

_____

_____

_____

_____

Chapter 6

Rob Anger Management Class

One day Trey and I decided to rob the anger management class where he was going for anger management. Trey had started smoking weed and drinking alcohol just like me. So, to support our habit we set up an armed robbery which included me holding up the counselor with a knife. Trey and his girlfriend dropped me off around the corner from the anger management building and left to park on the next street. I ran up to the red brick building and slipped on my skully and pulled out my knife. I looked both ways and made sure no one was coming, then I ran inside the building. There was a heavyset Caucasian woman sitting behind the desk just like Trey had described to me.

There was a slim Caucasian guy sitting in front of her. I ran to the woman and put the knife to her neck and said, "empty out the register and give me all the money". "Ok please don't hurt me", she said. She was shaking as she emptied out the register and handed me over the cash. As she handed me the cash, the guy that was sitting in front of her seemed like he wanted to be a hero and tackle me to the ground. "Don't you move I'll cut her throat", I told him.

He eased back down in the seat. I ran out the building and around the back, jumped a few fences and met Trey and his girlfriend on the next block and jumped in the back seat. "You did it" asked Trey. "Yea, she was scared!" "I told you they had money in there", Trey said. "Heck yea", I replied. Trey girlfriend drove off and we went straight to the weed man. After purchasing some weed we went and brought some alcohol and went to Trey girlfriend house and divided the cash, and got drunk and high that night.

What did you learn? How will you implement?

_____

_____

_____

_____

_____

_____

_____

_____

_____

_____

_____

_____

_____

_____

_____

_____

_____

_____

_____

_____

_____

Chapter 7

Introduced to Crack

One day I went to my aunt's house, which was a yellow duplex with 3 rooms and a small kitchen and living room. My cousin Corn stayed with his mother. I went into his mother room where he kept his drugs in a safe and opened it up while he was gone. The safe was kind of easy because all you had to do was stick any key in it and it opened up. I grabbed a couple pieces of crack that looked like popcorn. That was the reason they called Corn, Corn, because of the way he cooked his crack. I closed the safe back how I found it and left out the room. I walked the down the hall, through the living room and left out the side door. No one was home at the time. I was living there off and on while living in the street from pillar to pole.

I walked a few blocks up to my homeboy Red house where I had been living also. Red was a short, light skinned, slim fellow with a high-top fade whom loved to laugh a lot and joke around like me. Red lived with his grandmother and had a lot of freedom to do what he wanted to do just like me. I walked in the door and went to the back room where Red was at laying in the bed talking on the phone. "Sup Red", I said. "What up K.O.", Red replied. "Everything bro, I got that work check it", I said. Red jumped up off the bed. "Hey let me call you back", Red told the person on the other line. "So, where it's at", said

Red. I pulled out an orange pill bottle that was halfway full of the white pieces of popcorn crack cocaine.

"Right here bruh", I replied! I opened up the pill bottle and poured out the crack cocaine on the dresser. "What's up cuz you ready to make some money", I asked Red. "Heck yea", said Red. "I'm going to give you half to sell and I'll sell half", I told Red as I separated the hard-white cocaine. Red gathered up his share of the crack and put it into a pill bottle he found in the bathroom cabinet. Red threw on some jeans and put his shoes on, then we made our way down the hall and out the front door.

Red and I walked up to the A&A which was a neighborhood store where all the drugs were sold and where the most crime took place. People were shot and killed up at this store for drug deals gone bad. We waited on the corner of A&A. A crack head walked around the corner looking to buy a dime piece of crack. Red and I raced across the parking lot in an attempt to get to the crack head first. I made it to the crack head first. I pulled out my capsule and poured out a dime and gave it to the crack head in exchange for a 10-dollar bill. After receiving the 10-dollar bill I knew this would be what I wanted to do for the rest of my life. To make money this easy was the best thing I had ever experienced. We stayed at the A&A all-day serving crack to crack heads and making money.

What did you learn? How will you implement?

_____

_____

_____

_____

_____

_____

_____

_____

_____

_____

_____

_____

_____

_____

_____

_____

_____

_____

_____

_____

_____

_____

_____

_____

_____

_____

_____

_____

_____

_____

_____

_____

_____

_____

_____

_____

_____

_____

_____

_____

_____

_____

_____

Chapter 8

Steal Car

As I started to sell crack on a small-scale nickel and diming on the corner, I started to get involved in more criminal activity. I had a friend named Spoke whom I had played minor league football with as a kid. Like me Spoke had chosen the criminal life and was a master at stealing cars. One day Spoke, Red, and I had got together to steal a car to joy ride in. Red and I knew nothing about stealing cars. Spoke knew everything about stealing cars. He taught us how to steal cars. Spoke broke out the back window with a flat head screw driver and unlocked the door. Spoke then unlocked our doors.

"Come on hurry up get in", yelled Spoke! Red and I jumped in. Spoke had the flat head screw driver chipping away around the steering wheel. Once Spoke had chipped away around the steering wheel he stuck the screw driver into the column of the steering wheel and pulled back and the car started up in a matter of seconds. Spoke was the quickest car jacker I had ever seen. We sped off down the road and we joy rode all night listening to music, smoking weed and drinking liquor like this was our very own car.

The next day we ditched that car because we knew the owners had probably called it in by now. Spoke had went his separate way from Red and I. So Red and I decided to steal another car since we had learned from Spoke how to do it. Later on that night Red and I went back out into this white neighborhood and stole another car. We rode out to E.G. which was a neighborhood on the north side of the city to meet some girls we had been dating. After leaving the girls house we went home and parked the stolen car in a safe place.

I had started going to J.R High school with Red to Central Jr High. We got up to go to school, got dressed and went out the door like we were going to the bus stop. Red and I went and got into the stolen car we had stolen the night before. We drove to school in the car and parked it in the parking lot like it was ours.

Red and I had gotten so good at stealing cars until we had a stolen car almost every night. We had started stealing separate cars for ourselves. One day Red and I decided to steal a car together again. We got into the car and chipped the steering wheel and crunk the car up. As we started to ride off we seen a cop coming down the street. As we passed by the cop, he looked at us and seen the broken window in the back and whipped his car around and got behind us.

"That pig done got behind us dang", said Red. "Don't worry about it I got this", I told Red. I stepped on the gas as the cop turned on his blue lights. I raced down University Blvd and made a left on Lipscomb. The cop was right on our trail. "Turn here", said Red. I turned and the car was on two wheels as I bent the corner. The car landed back on all four as I raced through the stop signs with the cops right on our trail. By now there was back up that had joined the high-speed chase. As I raced through the neighborhoods, I came up on the graveyard.

I excelled through the graveyard with the cops behind us. As I got ready to bend the corner I told Red to get ready to jump out the car. I bent the corner and Red and I jumped out of the car at the same time and took off on feet as the car rolled and slammed into the wall. Now Red and I was starting athletes on the minor league football teams as kids, we both played running back positions so the chances of the cops catching us on foot running behind us was slim to none. We split up, Red went one way and I went the other way. We out ran the cops and got away. We met back up at the house later on that night and talked and laughed about we both escaped.

What did you learn? How will you implement?

_____

_____

_____

_____

_____

_____

_____

_____

_____

_____

_____

_____

_____

_____

_____

_____

_____

_____

_____

_____

Chapter 9

County Jail

A group of friends and I decided to walk to Fee Ave pool. Which was a pool on the other side of town outside of the urban area. I had decided to take a gun with me that I had come across a few days earlier. As we left out of booker heights the neighborhood I lived in, we came upon an empty field. While we walked across the empty field I pulled out the hand gun out my waist and started firing it up in the air to test it out to see what I was working with. Pow! Pow! Pow! The gun had a powerful kick and was very loud.

"Dang, this gun loud and it got a powerful kick", I said. I put the gun back in my waist and we came upon a suburban area. As we walked through the suburban area and started to cross the street we were met by the Melbourne Police Department. "Where you guys going", said the officer. "We're walking to the pool", I told the officer.

The officer looked at us all. We all were black teenagers. "I received a call of gun shots in the area", said the officer. "I'm going to need you all to stand beside each other in a straight line so I can pat you down", said the officer. We all got in a straight-line side by side like the officer had requested. My heart was beating fast and sweat was coming down my face because I was strapped with the gun he was looking for that the people in the suburban area had complained about hearing gun shots from.

The officer started to pat us down from left to right. As the officer got close I began to get nervous because I knew if this officer gets to me and pats me down I'm going to jail and jail was not the place I wanted to go at 16 years old. As the officer approached me after patting down 3 members of the crew, I braced myself and decided to make a run for it when the officer got to me.

With every passing moment my heart started to beat faster. As the officer approached me and asked me to put my hands in the air so he could search me, I knew this was the moment. It was either get caught with this gun and go to jail, or make a dash for it through the college campus we were stopped in front of. "Put", before the officer could finish the sentence I took off running towards the college campus. I could hear the officer behind me yelling "stop"! I kept running fast as I could. As I approached the wooded area I could hear the officer behind me on his walkie talkie calling it in, "We have a black male on foot armed and dangerous", he said as he kept running after me.

I came upon this bridge in the wooded area and crossed over it. I was scared and breathing hard with sweat pouring down my face from the hot Florida beaming sun. As I made a turn off the bridge onto the college campus I slung the gun into the wooded area to keep from getting caught with it. Once on the college campus cops were everywhere, the cop that was chasing me had called in for backup. "Get on the ground", a cop shouted as he jumped out his car in front of me with his weapon drawn.

I was tired and exhausted. I had gotten rid of the gun so there was no need for me to run any further. The only reason I had ran anyway was to get rid of the gun so I wouldn't be caught with it. I already knew I would go to jail if I was caught with it. "Get on the ground", the cop shouted again, breathing hard sweat pouring down my face, knees weak and about to buckle from all the running, I couldn't go another step. I put my hands up in the air and got on the ground.

The cops rushed me as I got on the ground, one put his knee in my back, handcuffed me, searched me and then threw me in the back seat of the police car. "Where did you throw the gun", one cop asked. "I don't know what you are talking about", I replied. "The gun you had in your possession", said the cop. "I didn't have a gun", I told the cop. "Well why did you run", asked the cop? "I was scared", I replied. "If you weren't guilty of anything you had no reason to run", the cop told me. "Police kill innocent blacks every day, I was scared for my life", I said. The cop face was turning red as he got angrier because I wouldn't tell him where I threw the gun. The cop slammed the door of the back seat of the police car where I was handcuffed and walked away.

About an hour later the police returned to the police car after a massive search of the wooded area with the news they had found the gun. "We found the gun and you are being charged with aggravated assault on a police officer, resisting arrest and possession of a stolen fire arm", said the officer. I was only 16 years old and facing charges like these, all because I ran to get rid of the gun I didn't want to get caught with it. The police had lied and said I pointed the gun at him while I was throwing the gun away. After reading me my rights, they drove me away in the police car to the Melbourne Police Department.

After going to the Melbourne Police Department, I was sent to the detention center the same day. I spent a couple weeks in the detention center and later was adjudicated as an adult and sent to the county jail. Inside the county jail adjudicated as an adult, I was placed with other teenagers that had been adjudicated as an adult. They fed us three times a day and allowed us to take a shower once a day. The juveniles were wild. There were fights almost every day and inmates would choke each other out in fights. Choking another person out in a fight had become a normal thing. When you fought you couldn't let the other opponent get a hold around your neck or he would put you to sleep. You had to be tough and not be a wimp. If you were inmates would sense your fear then you would become a target. After six months of incarceration I went to trial and beat the case. I was released from jail to the custody of my aunt Cathy who had been to coming to trial with me.

What did you learn? How will you implement?

_____

_____

_____

_____

_____

_____

_____

_____

_____

_____

_____

_____

_____

_____

_____

_____

_____

_____

_____

Chapter 10

Aunt Cathy

I lived with aunt Cathy for a few months after registering in Southwest Junior High School. I signed up to play football, but ended up quitting to continue boxing. I spent most of my time at Red house, so my aunt Cathy gave me the option to live with Red and his grandmother if I wanted to. I took the option because Red lived in the hood in a neighborhood known as Booker Heights where I spent my teenage years with my family off and on. I eventually quit boxing also. Red and I had gotten real close and were like family. His grandmother was my grandmother and his family was mine. Red had a cousin I was introduced to named lil daddy.

Lil daddy was a short browned skinned man with dark wavy hair and a muscular build. In the hood we all had crazy nick names. Lil daddy and I had gotten real close just like Red and I was. Lil daddy was older than Red and I. He introduced us to a life of crime we had never seen before. Along with the petty hustling we were doing selling crack cocaine, we started to snort coke and stay up all night looking for crimes to get into. While intoxicated with drugs we would set up armed robberies robbing drug dealers and convenience stores. We had discovered a passion for breaking into people houses when they were not home.

We would steal guns, jewelry, money and whatever we could find in these houses. Lil daddy had a girlfriend name Lisa who was friends with a lady named lady J whom I was attracted to. Lady J was a short browned skinned sexy beautiful woman that wore a short haircut with one gold in her mouth and she was thick and fine! I told Lil daddy to have Lisa put a bug in Lady J ear for me and she did! One day Lady J came down to the house while I was there. She knocked on the door and came in. Lil daddy, Lisa, Red and I was sitting in the living room smoking weed.

"Hey how ya'll doing", she asked? "Shoot smoking", Lil daddy replied. "Want to hit the blunt?" Lil daddy asked her. "Sure", she replied. Lil daddy passed her the blunt. Lady J sat down beside me. "It's Ok if I sit here?" she asked "Sure", I replied. "Lisa told me you asked about me", she said. "Oh yea", I replied. "Yes", she said with a smile on her face. "So, your name is Kent?", she asked? "Yes, my name is Kent", I replied. "And you are Lady J correct?"

"Yes, I'm lady J", she said as she grinned. "So how old are you?", she asked. I knew that she was a lot older than me because Lil daddy had told me she had a son that wasn't too far behind me in age. He had told me she was 28. I had to come up with a lie to keep her from turning me down. I was only 17, but I couldn't let her know I was a minor. "I'm 19", I replied. "19"?

She asked again in excitement as she was caught off guard by my answer. "Yes", I responded. "How old are you may I ask"? I asked her. I'm 28. "Well age isn't nothing but a number", I said. "Well I guess so, as long as your over 18 I can't get in any trouble", she said. "Well do you mind if we exchange numbers", I asked? "No I don't mind, my number is 321-704-3388", she said. "Mine is 321-604-0150", I told her. We hung out all night at Lil daddy house laughing and smoking weed. As day break came in, Lady J went home and I passed out on Lil daddy couch.

What did you learn? How will you implement?

Chapter 11

Set-up by Police

Lady J and I had become real close as boyfriend and girlfriend. Lady J loved me and I loved her a lot. Lady J was from the streets and she knew about selling drugs just as much as I did. She would take me to make drug transactions. She would do anything for me. One day I got a page on my beeper from a customer that placed an order for a $40 piece of crack cocaine which was 2 dime rocks when sold to a Caucasian customer. I didn't know the guy who had beep me and ordered the $40 piece of crack but I took down his request.

One rule of the drug game was to never sell drugs to someone you don't know because they could be the police. Lady J drove me to meet the customer at the 7 Eleven convenience store. There was A white heavy-set man with a dirty brown and gray santa claus looking beard standing beside the pay phone when we pulled up. "What's up", I whispered out the car window. He came to the car and got in the back seat. I reached back and gave him the $40 piece of crack. "Put it in you mouth and taste it", I told him. I wanted to be sure he wasn't the police.

After he acted like he didn't want to put the crack in his mouth I snatched It from him. "Get out my car", I yelled. He opened the door and got out. I knew something wasn't right about this whole thing. We backed up and pulled out of the parking lot onto the highway and was stopped by a red light. Then out of nowhere came red and blue lights. Police men jumped out their cars with their guns drawn. "Put the car in park and put your hands up", they yelled. Lady J put the car in park. "K.O. give me your dope", said Lady J. I gave her the dope right before they told me to get out the car.

They threw me up against the car and began to search me. "Where's the drugs", said the officer that was patting me down. He was a slim tall officer with blond hair, blue eyes and a clean shave. "I don't know what you're talking about", I told the officer. "You know what I'm talking about, the crack you just tried to sell to officer John", he screamed! "I didn't try to sell officer John anything", I replied. The officers made me take off my shoes and socks as they searched me intensively.

After realizing I didn't have anything on me, they put me in the police car. Then they went over to the driver side where Lady J was sitting. Lady J knew they were on their way to harass her. Lady J put the small bag of crack in her mouth to hide it. The cops asked Lady J to step out of the car. Lady J stepped out the car. Once Lady J was out the car the cop began to search her. "Where's the drugs your boyfriend had", asked the cop. "He didn't have any drugs", said Lady J.

"You're lying, we know he had drugs on him because he tried to sell it to our officer and you were there", screamed the officer. "I don't know what you're talking about sir", Lady J replied. The officer searched her up and down. All of a sudden, I heard the officer scream, "She's trying to swallow it"! As I look to the side out of the police car window, I could see the police with his hands around Lady J neck squeezing it trying to keep her from swallowing the drugs.

"Don't swallow it, don't you swallow it", the officer kept screaming. I could see Lady J was in pain as the officer held on to her throat harder to keep her from swallowing the drugs. I screamed from the back of the police car as I was handcuffed with my hands behind my back. "You're going to kill her, stop choking her," I screamed! "Stop it", I screamed louder. The cop kept a tight grip as tears started to roll down Lady J eyes as she swallowed the drugs.

After a few minutes of wrestling with Lady J trying to stop her from swallowing the drugs, the cop took his hand from around her throat. Lady J gasped for breath as she stood there winded trying to catch her breath. "She swallowed the drugs", said the officer. "We're going to have to have her stomach pumped out", the officer radioed in. They put Lady J in the other police car and took us off to jail.

What did you learn? How will you implement?

_____

_____

_____

_____

_____

_____

_____

_____

_____

_____

_____

_____

_____

_____

_____

_____

_____

_____

_____

_____

_____

_____

Chapter 12

Break In House

After a few days in Jail lady J and I was released back into society. Lil daddy and I had hooked back up. I was broke and didn't want to sell anymore drugs at the moment, being that I was just setup a few weeks ago by the police. Lil daddy and I decided to break into someone's house to put some money in our pockets. We knew exactly what to do because we had done it plenty of times before in the past. I picked lil daddy up at his house at 10am in my red four door Buick. "What up lil daddy", I said as he opened the door and got into the front seat. "Chilling cuz", you ready to get this money?" lil daddy replied. "Yea let's do it!" I said. We drove out to Palm Bay where most of the Caucasian population lived. Palm Bay was the city next to Melbourne, Fl., where I grew up.

We circled the neighborhood looking for the perfect house to break into. Once we spotted the house we thought would have the most valuable merchandise in it, we pulled into the two-car driveway. "Go and knock on the door", said Lil daddy. "Ok", I replied. I put the car in park and got out. As I walked up to the house I examined it. It was a white and brown one-story house with one living room window and two bedroom windows. The house looked like it was just built. As I continued to walk up I noticed through the blinds on the living room window there wasn't anyone in the house, at least as far as I could see. I walked up to the front door and knocked on it to be sure. No one answered. I knocked a little harder.

No one answered. I knocked a little harder just to be sure no one heard my knocks. If someone was there and would have heard my knocks I would have asked for someone I know that I knew would not have lived there and simply said I had the wrong house when they said no one lives here by that name. I turned around and walked back to the car. I opened up the door and got in and closed the door. "There's no one there", said lil daddy. "No sir", I replied. "Ok good, lets circle the block and find a place to park", lil daddy suggested. I put the car in reverse since I never turned it off and backed up out the driveway.

I circled the block and found a place to park my car in an apartment complex not to far from the house where we had knocked on the door. We got out and walked to the back of the house. Lil daddy used a screwdriver to take the master bedroom window that was in the back of the house out the frame and then he climbed in. After he was in I climbed in after him. Upon entering we noticed the house was a person or families house that had been in the military, because of the certificates and awards that had been hanging on the hallway wall straight ahead.

We looked intensively. After five minutes of searching the house lil daddy screamed, "K.O. check this out bra!" I came into the room where lil daddy was. "Boy we hit the jack pot", says lil daddy as he pointed to the closet. As I looked inside the closet it was full of guns that looked like guns people used in the army and marines. A-R 15's and glock nines. "Whoo hoo!" I yelled.

"Now this what I'm talking about, we in there now!" I said. "Grab as much as you can and let's get out of here", lil daddy told me. I grabbed as many guns as I could and went back out the back window and made my way to the car.

As I was headed back to the house lil daddy was coming out the window with the guns he had grabbed and was headed to the car. I got back into the window and grabbed a few miscellaneous things and made my way back to the car. After loading up everything we had grabbed out the house we headed home to take an inventory on everything we had stolen.

What did you learn? How will you implement?

_____

_____

_____

_____

_____

_____

_____

_____

_____

_____

_____

_____

_____

_____

_____

_____

_____

_____

_____

_____

_____

Chapter 13

Menace to Society

The block was thick there were people everywhere. Lil daddy and I pulled up in my Buick. My Buick was a four-door car with a maroon paint job with shiny chrome rims on it and a lot of music in it. My car was a dope boy car. Lil daddy and I pulled up to Cleo's, parked the car and hopped out. We walked up to the front of Cleo's and went inside. Cleo's was an old broken down night bar where lots of people hung out on the weekends.

We grabbed us some Hennessey and went back to my car to roll up an El product-o blunt to smoke. After fixing our cups of Hennessey and having a few drinks, lil daddy took out the bag of weed and started to roll up the blunt. As lil daddy rolled up the blunt a black van pulled up beside us and a crack head leaned out the passenger window and asked if we had a 20 piece of crack cocaine we could sell him. I always kept a pill bottle of crack cocaine on me and stayed ready. I walked up to the van, "what's up", I asked? "Let me get two dimes", he said. I pulled out my capsule of crack and poured out two-dime rocks and stuck it into the window and put it in the crack head hands.

The crack head took it and put half of one of the pieces of crack in his mouth to taste it, to make sure it was real. As he tasted it, the van begun to pull off slowly. I started to walk beside the van thinking it just was rolling. As it picked up a little speed I started to yell at the crack head, "Yo stop give me my money", I screamed. As I started to run on the side of the van yelling in the window! The van gained more speed. That's how I knew they were robbing me for my drugs at this point. I ran back to my car where lil daddy was. "Man them crack heads took my dope", I yelled to lil daddy!

"What, hell nah, where they went?", asked lil daddy "Hop in", I yelled!. Lil daddy hopped in and I sped off after the van. A few blocks down the road we rolled up on the van stopped at a stop sign. I parked and hopped out. I grabbed my 25-piece hand gun and lil daddy and I ran up to the passenger side of the vehicle. "Where is my dope", I yelled at the crack head that took the dope from me? "I don't have it, he has it", as he pointed to the driver. "I don't care who has it, I want my dope, or give me my money", I yelled.

"I don't have it man, he has your dope", he kept saying as he pointed to the driver. "Well I gave it to you, so you better come up with it", I screamed at the passenger! The two crack heads got out the car and started fighting each other. The one that took my dope ended up beating up the other one, which was the driver. "Hell nah", I yelled! "I want my dope", I screamed at the crack head that had taken my drugs. "Man I don't have it", he yelled!

I punched him with a right to the jaw, but didn't knock him down. He stumbled as he caught his balance and took off running. Lil daddy and I took off behind him chasing after him. I pulled out my 25 automatic and started firing it at him as we chased him across the street. He fell to the ground as he made it across the road. Lil daddy and I ran up to him. I pointed the gun at him while he laid on the ground and started to fire shots into his flesh hitting him in the stomach and chest area while I screamed at him for robbing me.

Every time I pulled the trigger the gun would jam. It would fire after pulling it twice. I shot him a couple times then lil daddy and I jumped in my Buick and sped off down the road. As we made it back to grandma house where we all hung out, I was furious. "Hell nah", I said! "I want to go back and finish him off", I yelled! I knew he wasn't dead, and I was still mad because of how he tried me and I couldn't let him get away with it.

I wanted to make an example out of him for anyone else that wanted to rob me. Lil daddy and I hopped back into my car and headed back over to where I had shot the crack head. As we approached the area where I shot the crack head we saw him staggering down the sidewalk by the blue apartments, which was some low-income apartment complexes. We hopped out and ran up to him.

Still furious I screamed, "You're going to pay for what you did", I yelled! "Come on man, you done shot me and beat me up", what else you're going to do", he yelled! "Now you're going to die", I screamed as we beat him down with our fist and kicking him to sleep. After beating and kicking him we jumped back into my Buick and sped off once again.

What did you learn? How will you implement?

_____

_____

_____

_____

_____

_____

_____

_____

_____

_____

_____

_____

_____

_____

_____

_____

_____

_____

_____

_____

_____

_____

_____

_____

_____

_____

_____

_____

_____

_____

_____

_____

_____

_____

_____

_____

_____

_____

_____

_____

_____

_____

_____

_____

_____

_____

_____

_____

_____

_____

Chapter 14

Repercussion

Several months later after pawning some of the stolen merchandise we had stolen out of the houses we had broken into, I was stopped by the Melbourne Police Department for speeding. I pulled over under a street light as the red and blue lights and sirens echoed shining through the night. As the police got out of the car my heart started to beat fast, because I didn't know if my license was suspended or not, plus you never knew what a white cop would do to a black man.

The cop was a white older male about six feet tall, fat with a big gut, hairy looking fellow with bifocal glasses on that made his eyes look gigantic. He walked up to the side of my car, I made sure I had my seat belt on then I rolled down the window. "License and registration please", said the officer as he shinned his flashlight in my face. "Sir what did you pull me for?" I asked him. "You were going 55 in a 45 mph zone", said the officer. "I was only going 48 sir", I replied. "I clocked you going 55, license and registration", he said again a little more aggressively.

I sighed and reached into the glove department as the officer watched me with his hands on his weapon making sure I wasn't reaching for a weapon inside the glove department. He was a nasty officer too, I could tell from the way he was responding, that if I would have made any false move I would have been dead. I grabbed the registration and my wallet out the glove department very slowly and handed him my license out my wallet along with the registration. He grabbed my information, "I'm going to run your license and registration, if everything looks good I'll write you a ticket for speeding and let you be on your way", he said. "Ok", I replied.

The officer walked away back to his police car and got in. While I waited for the police to return it felt like eternity. I started shaking a little in fear, because after all of the crimes and things I had done in my life as a juvenile, I never knew what to expect. As I sat there shaking playing with my fingers I kept looking out my side and rearview mirror for the cop to return. All I could think about is I hope my license is good. I grabbed the bottle of coke I had in the cup holder and took a sip, then sat it back down.

After about a half hour of sitting in the car waiting for this cop to come back with my paperwork, two more cops pulled up behind him. The first cop got out. He was a white male seemed to be in his thirties with blond hair. He stood about 5'9 in height and 180 pounds with a long nose. The second cop to arrive after him got out his car.

He was also a white male with brown hair, he was about 6 feet in height. I could see all three officers out my mirrors as they gathered there up under the streetlight discussing something. I didn't have a clue what was going on and what they were discussing. All of a sudden all three officers began to walk towards my car with their hands on their weapons. They didn't draw their guns, but they made sure they had their hands on them.

As they got closer to the car my heart felt like it wanted to jump out my chest as I started to shake and as sweat started to pour down my face. I had just heard about my boy Mark Ford being killed by this white cop in my neighborhood. I knew white cops could be racist. I knew this wasn't going to end well. I placed both hands on the steering wheel as they walked up to the back of my car. One officer went to the passenger side of my car and two walked up on the driver side.

All three cops had their flashlights out flashing inside my car. As the officers made their way to both windows, "Sir please step out the car there's a warrant out for your arrest", says the first officer who had pulled me over. "For what, I didn't do anything!" I said angrily. "Sir please step out the car and place your hands behind your back", the cop demanded. I got out the car and turned around with my chest to the back window and put my hands behind my back. "You are being charged with 3 counts of dealing in stolen property and violation of probation", said the officer.

The officer began to read me my rights, "You have the right to remain silent. If you do say anything, what you say can be used against you in the court of law. You have the right to consult with a lawyer and have that lawyer present during any questioning. If you cannot afford a lawyer, one will be appointed for you if you so desire". Once the arresting officer was finished reading me my rights, which was the cop that had pulled me over, they walked me to the back of the police car and put me in the back seat.

After a few minutes of them talking among themselves in front of the arresting officer police car, the arresting officer got in the car and drove me off to the Melbourne Police Department.

What did you learn? How will you implement?

_____

_____

_____

_____

_____

_____

_____

_____

_____

_____

_____

_____

_____

_____

_____

_____

_____

_____

_____

_____

_____

_____

_____

_____

_____

_____

_____

_____

_____

_____

_____

_____

_____

_____

_____

_____

_____

_____

_____

_____

_____

_____

_____

_____

_____

_____

Chapter 15

Sentenced To Prison 2 Years

In 1998 at 19 years old I was sentenced to two years in prison. One morning in the Brevard county jail about 4am in the morning while I was laying in my bunk I heard CO's call my name over the intercom to pack it up I was on my way. I knew what that meant, because I had then heard that come over the intercom several times before when other inmates were on their way to prison at the Orange County Reception Center in Orlando, Fl. better known as O.C.I. I packed my things and made my way to the metal sliding door that kept us inmates confined in this huge dormitory.

The dormitory we were housed in was huge. It was shaped like a triangle with red bricks. It had two floors with several rooms upstairs and downstairs. There were several gray tables with stools attached to them for dining. There was one TV that sat high on the wall and a few phones that were used to make calls at certain times. There were showers on each end of the rooms on both floors, four showers in all and about 40 rooms with bunk beds in each dormitory.

It would get so packed people had to sleep on the floors in the dormitory on mats. In each room were two bunks with a stainless stool and sink. There was also a small window you could look out of. The ground was cement no carpet. The jail would get so packed that people would have to sleep on floors in the rooms also, which were already small rooms. There were several fights that broke out. While I was there I wasn't involved in any. While I waited by the sliding door for it to open, it soon opened up. I walked out and was joined with several other inmates.

We were walked down the hall by the CO and took to a holding cell. After several hours in the holding cell, we were shackled, then put in deputy vans and escorted to the Orange County Reception Center. It was a short thirty-minute ride. Upon entering the reception center I noticed the huge gates made of barbed wire fences with tall towers. They housed armed guards to secure the perimeter, just in case some inmate or inmates tried to escape. There was also an armed guard that drove around the perimeter.

After entering and clearing the first set of gates, we were pulled into a big garage. I climbed out the van all shackled up. I was led inside this holding cell where I was unchained, stripped and searched intensively. After making me hold my private and bending over to cough while I was naked, I was sent to a barber to have my head shaved bald. They made me do all of that to make sure I didn't have anything placed in my anus.

After that I had to take a shower and was given a blue prison uniform to put on. After the intake process was done I was sent to my dorm. On the way to the dorm I noticed how huge this prison was as I stepped in the compound. The compound was the yard where all the criminals hung out. There were basketball goals, weights, commissary booths, baseball fields and barbershops. The grass was green and there were yellow lines on the concrete that had to be utilized by inmates for feeding and inmate control. I made my way across the compound escorted by the CO and entered my dorm room where I would be living at until I was done with the reception process. The dorms were similar to the county jail dorms.

The reception process usually took 2-3 months of medical clearances, blood test, a little schooling, ect. It was a process that had to be done before each inmate was sent to a permanent camp. After about 2 months at the Orange County Reception Center I was transported on the Blue Bird to Butler Correctional Institution. The Blue Bird was the name of the bus that the prisons moved the inmates on. Butler Correctional Institution was just a transitional facility, so I wasn't there long.

After one day at Butler Correctional Institution I was transferred again, this time the ride was a long ride, unlike the ride from Brevard County Jail. The ride to Butler C.I. seemed like it took forever. I looked out the windows of the Blue Bird at the trees and grassy hills to pass time. After several hours, we were almost to Alabama when we pulled up to Jackson Correctional Institution. This would be my permanent home for the next year and 10 months. Department Of Corrections had sent me so far from home I couldn't believe it! How was I going to see anybody and have visits, I thought to myself.

The bus pulled in through the entrance of the barbed wire fence. The bus was searched underneath and around. The driver drove into inmate receiving where I went through a small intake process that was much smaller than O.C.I. Once I was done with the intake process and placed in my room where I would be for the remaining of my stay, I just laid back on my bed with my chest facing the ceiling. I just took that time to reflect how good it really felt to be locked away in prison. I felt like being incarcerated saved me.

I was tired and my body was tired. All the powder I had been snorting, drinking, smoking weed, robing, stealing and snatching purses hurt me. I really needed this vacation to think about some things. Like how my life was going nowhere fast and spiraling down at a tremendous pace. After all the things I went through, I could have been dead. After thinking about all these things and being saved from the streets by being incarcerated, I started to make myself comfortable.

I was placed at the work camp of Jackson C.I. where I was able to go out and work for gain time, which was days off my sentence for working and good behavior. At Jackson C.I. like all prisons, we would have to take showers together. There were rows of showerheads in the shower and inmates would get in next to each other and take showers. I never did like the fact of being butt naked taking showers with other men, but this was the system.

Inmates would get in the shower right next to you and masturbate while watching the woman officer through the glass who was on duty. If an inmate got caught doing that he was placed in solitary confinement for several days. Some inmates didn't care, they waited right until an officer looked their way and they gunned her down. I guess it was something special when you and the female officer make contact while you're masturbating.

Gunned down was another word for masturbation when you are looking at a female officer, or if you were gay it was when you look at a man officer. I never participated in the whole gunning down process, but I did have my masturbation moments. I spent most of my time working out. I had also developed a passion for writing rap music, which I loved to listen to when I was free. Tupac Shakur was my favorite rapper.

There was a guy I met at Jackson C.I. by the name of D-Dub. D-Dub and I use to write raps and perform them in the rec. yard. Inmates would gather around as D-Dub would beat on the tables making gangster beats. Him and I would rap to them. We made a name for our selves around the work camp rapping. Everyday after work we would go out on the rec. yard and rap. Guys would tell me all the time, "Kent when you get out don't let it go bruh, don't let it go". "I won't",

I would tell them. I would have to go out on the road crew to Tallahassee, Fl and chop trees and pickup trash. One day I was out on the road crew in Tallahassee, Fl and came up on a hive of yellow jacket bees in the ground. When I chopped the tree they came out and I was stung above the eye. The next day my eye was so fat it looked like I had been in a fistfight. I was in pain. After several days the swelling went down and I was right back out there on the road crew. After a year and a half counting down the days and months at Jackson C.I. I was sent to work release.

Work release allowed me to go to work with the public to transition me back to society. When I was in work release I would call home. I was able to contact a cousin of mine by the name of biggie. Before I got locked up Biggie was a small time hustler trying to break into the dope game. Biggie was a big black fellow that would put you in the mind of the rapper Biggie Smalls. Biggie wasn't a popular guy, when he would try to speak to woman they wouldn't give him the time of day.

He didn't wear the best of clothes and always looked run down with his pants hanging off showing the crease between his buttocks. He was always a little musky from the weight he carried. He didn't wear name brand shoes. Biggie grew up poor, never had any money. Biggie was a year younger than me. "Hello", said Biggie as he answered the phone. "What up cuz", I replied. "Who is this? K.O.?" Said Biggie in his deep voice. "Yea this me cuz, what it do fam?" I asked. "Boy it's good to hear your voice"! Said Biggie.

We been waiting on you to come home, things not like it use to be, your lil cuz done came up!" Said Biggie "When you coming home boy?" Biggie asked. I got 2 months left, I replied. "Well when you get out make sure you hit me up, I'm not going talk too much on the phone, but listen its good hearing your voice and we can't wait until you come home", biggie said with excitement!

"Neither can I cuz, listen when I touchdown I'm going to hit you", I said excitingly! I knew from how he was talking I was fixing to be put on when I got out the pin. "Alright cuz hold it down in there and I'll see you soon", said Biggie! "Alright cuz", I replied then I hung up the phone. I went back to my room happy as a clam because it was about to be on once I was free.

What did you learn? How will you implement?

Chapter 16

Free At Last

July 2, 2001, fresh out of prison! My girl met me at the bus station, as I got off the bus she ran up and swung her arms around me and gave me a big hug! "Hey baby I'm so glad you are free", said Lady J. "So am I, that place was horrible", I replied. "Let's get out of here, I'm hungry, I want some real food"! I said. "Where do you want to go baby", said lady J. "I want some Lobster, steak, or shrimp", I suggested.

I had a few dollars saved up in my account from work release, but I knew Lady J would hold me down for now until I could get on my feet. After being home a few days spending time with Lady J making up for lost time, I knew it was time to get on the grind and make me some money. I was almost broke. I called up Biggie. "What up family, I'm out"! I said. "O yea!" Said Biggie excitingly. "When you got out boy?", said Biggie. "I been out for a few days, just been chilling with my girl making up for lost time", I replied. "I want to come through and holler at ya", it's been a while since we chilled, shoot me your address", I said. "Yea boy come through, I'll text you my address", said Biggie.

"Alright cool", I replied then hung up the phone. I had lady J to take me around to Biggie apartment in the hood. Biggie was living in an apartment complex that had been a known drug area, but Biggie was only here so he could come up in the drug game. When you in the drug game you start off small, low key and cheap. You don't want to be flashy because when you are trying to come up, you got to stay below the radar. We pulled up to the back of the apartments where everybody parked. I got out and went and knocked on the back door.

"Who is it"? Asked a voice on the other side. "It's K.O.", I replied. Biggie girlfriend Mitch answered the door. Mitch was Caucasian, about 5'5 in height, 130 pounds, brown eyes and long brown hair. "Hey K.O.!" "Come in", said Mitch. "How's it going Mitch", I replied as I entered through the door. "Everything is going great"!

"Biggie is upstairs, give me a minute, I'll run upstairs and get him", said Mitch. As Mitch made her way down the hall and up the stairs, I pulled out one of the chairs from around the dining room table and sat in it. I looked around the small apartment kitchen at the stove, cabinets and refrigerator. It didn't look brand-new they were very used.

These apartments weren't places to live for the rest of your life, only used for a trap house. After a few minutes I could hear the stairs as they cracked as biggie made his way down them and into the kitchen where I was sitting. "What up boy", said Biggie with a huge smile on his face as he greeted me with a warm brotherly hug. "What's up with ya", I replied? "I'm glad to be home!"

I said. "Yea I feel ya", said Biggie as he grabbed a ounce of weed out the cabinets and tossed it to me. "You still remember how to roll up don't you", Biggie asked with a smile on his face. "Heck yea", I replied as Biggie also was tossing me the el producto blunt to roll the weed up with. After rolling up the blunt, Biggie had me to follow him in the living room. Once inside the living room, I sat down on the couch.

Biggie sat down on the couch in front of me. "Mitch bring down that red Jordan shoe box in the closet that's sitting on the shelf", yelled Biggie to Mitch who was upstairs. A couple minutes later Mitch came down stairs with the red Jordan shoebox he had asked for. Mitch handed Biggie the shoebox. Biggie took the shoebox and placed it on the table that sat between us. Biggie opened up the shoebox and pulled out 5 circles of crack cocaine that was shaped like a chocolate chip cookie. Some had already been broken and some was still a full circle.

"You think you can get rid a couple of these", asked Biggie? "No doubt", I replied. "You already know I can, I make money", I said. "I'm going to give you two of them, just bring me back $500", said Biggie. "Ok cool, soon as I sell these two I'll be right back to grab two more", I said. "Yea that's what I'm talking about", said Biggie.

"You keep getting rid of them I'll keep supplying you more, it won't be a thing", said Biggie. "As you see I have plenty where that came from", Biggie said as he smiled and puffed the blunt. We sat in the living room talking and catching up on old times as we smoked, laughed and played John madden football on the PlayStation for the next couple hours until it was time for me to go home.

I called Lady J to come pick me up. About 15 minutes later Lady J was at the door knocking to pick me up. Biggie and I got up and shook hands. "Alright boy I'll get up with you later", said Biggie as I opened and exited out the back door with the two cookies of crack cocaine wrapped in a napkin in a paper plate. "Alright cuz I'll check you later", I said as I opened the car door and sat inside. Lady J backed up and we went home.

What did you learn? How will you implement?

_____

_____

_____

_____

_____

_____

_____

_____

_____

_____

_____

_____

_____

_____

_____

_____

_____

_____

_____

_____

_____

Chapter 17

Move In With Biggie

Lady J and I had gotten into an argument. She was upset because I was spending a lot of time over at Biggie house and accused me of being with other women. She had threatened to take my car that was in her name. When I was in prison she had put my car in her name and used it to get around which I was fine with. One day when she wasn't home I hired a crack head that knew how to fix cars to come take the engine out of it so she couldn't drive it since she wanted to be nasty, plus that was an expensive engine I had in there.

One day when she walked outside to get into the car, the car wouldn't start. She lifted up the hood to see why the car wouldn't start, there was no engine underneath. She was surprised an angry. She called me immediately and threatened to call the cops on me. I didn't care because it was my car and she knew it. After the threat she didn't call the cops. I moved in with Biggie. Once I had moved in with Biggie the sky was the limit. Weed, coke, alcohol was our lifestyle.

We would get up every morning roll up a blunt and smoke. Then we would get into Biggie car which was a chevy impala sitting on twenty-two's with major bang, 8 twelve's in the back of the trunk and Tv's in it. Biggie would ride with cookies of crack cocaine stacked in a paper plate most of the times to make deliveries. I would only carry a small amount unless it was ordered for me to bring more. One day I called D-Dub on the phone whom I had been locked up in prison with. "What up D-Dub?" I said as he answered the phone.

"What up who is this?", asked D-Dub "This your boy K.O. from prison, dang homie you don't remember my voice", I asked. "O K.O. what's going on homie", he said excitingly! "Nothing much big dawg, wanted to come through and holler at ya", I said. "Sure come on through, it's been a lil minute, I'll be glad to see you", said D-Dub. "I need your address", I said. D-Dub read out his address as I wrote it down.

"What time you planning on coming?", said D-Dub. "I'm going to leave in the morning", I replied. "Alright then", said D-Dub. "Alright I'll see you then", I said as I hung up the phone. D-Dub had the connect on supplying me with some ex-pills I could sell. The next day I borrowed biggie's rental car and left to go to visit D-Dub in Tampa, Fl.

On the way I stopped by the liquor store and grabbed some hennessy. I took a few ex-pills along with me for the ride. I swallowed one of the pills, rolled me a blunt and fixed me a cup of hennessy and started to drive to Tampa. As I made my way down the highway on I-4 in Polk County, I was speeding and was pulled over by the sheriff. I instantly let down my window to let all the smoke out of the car while I was being pulled so the sheriff wouldn't smell it.

The sheriff got out his car and walked up to the passenger side of my car. He was a white male in his mid 30's with brown eyes and brown hair. He was slim and tall. "License and registration", says the cop. "Sir what did you pull me for", I asked. "You were going 85 in a 70 mile zone", said the officer. As I reached in the glove compartment for the registration the cop asked, "Is there anything illegal in the car sir?". "No sir", I replied.

I handed the cop my license and registration and he walked back to his car. After several minutes another patrol car pulled up with his red and blue lights on. Then he got out. He was a white male in his mid fifties with blonde hair and blue eyes and seemed to be 6 feet between 180-200 pounds. He walked up to the other officer as one made his way to the passenger side and the other came to the driver side. I had seen this several times dealing with police throughout my youthful years. Most times it didn't turn out right.

Once the officer on the driver side made it to my window he said, "Sir please step out the car". "Why officer", I asked.

"There's an open bottle in your car, plus we smell marijuana in your car", says the officer. How silly of me I thought as I took my seat belt off and exited the car. How could I be so silly to have that bottle in sight like that, I should have noticed that is all I kept thinking.

The cops handcuffed me and took me to the front of the police car while they searched my vehicle. I was hoping they wouldn't find anything because I had only been out of prison for a couple months. As they searched the car they ended up pulling out the open container, bag of weed and 2 ex-pills. The officer walked back to me and told me everything they found, then read me my rights. "You have the right to remain silent. If you do say anything, what you say can be used against you in the court of law.

You have the right to consult with a lawyer and have that lawyer present in any questioning. If you cannot afford a lawyer, one will be appointed for you if you so desire." After that I was put in the back of the police car and sent to jail in Polk County where I spent the next month in incarceration after getting out on time served and supervised probation. Biggie and his brother rental car was impounded which they accused me of stealing.

What did you learn? How will you implement?

Chapter 18

A Different Level

A year had passed since I had been released from the Polk County Jail and placed on probation. Biggie and I had moved to a different part of town known as Woodfield Apartment Complex. I had come up in the dope game and was making a very decent living off of it. You see once I got around Biggie and his brother half pint that is. They were about their business of making money and wasn't about that foolish life I was used to. Before going to prison, my mind frame and attitude started to change. I started to dress different, think different and act different. They say its levels to the game, which it really is.

I was fronting the dope from Biggie until I saved up enough to buy my own. Biggie and his brother half-pint who was short, brown skinned, with 18 gold teeth in his mouth, black hair, dark brown eyes and wore a short haircut was a team and always worked together. Biggie was the one that would sell all the dope and half-pint had the connection and would bring the dope in. They would often times get in physical fights and arguments behind their business. We were all getting money on different levels.

Biggie and Half-Pint would have cookies of crack laying around for customers to see when they walked in. I knew the dangers associated with letting customers see too much product, so I always moved in secret not letting my left hand know what my right hand was doing. Biggie would cook crack for anybody without knowing whom he could trust. He would charge them a small fee while they watched. I continued to buy cars for cheap and invested large amounts of money in them like I had done in the past before I went to prison.

I was into fixing up cars putting big rims, paint jobs, music, strong engines and brand new interior into them. I started to buy lots of jewelry and put more gold in my mouth. By the time I was finished putting gold teeth in my mouth I had 16 gold teeth. 8 to the top and 8 to the bottom. Biggie was into the same things now that he was on strong. We were real flashy when it came to luxury, maybe a little too flashy.

It was to the point everyone knew we were big time drug dealers because of our fancy lifestyles without a job. When people see you riding around all day with jewelry, gold teeth in your mouth and a hooked up ride they start to put 2 and 2 together. So the cops definitely used this to their advantage.

What did you learn? How will you implement?

_____

_____

_____

_____

_____

_____

_____

_____

_____

_____

_____

_____

_____

_____

_____

_____

_____

_____

_____

_____

Chapter 19

Jamerican Prince Is Born

As I started to make more money I began to invest in producing music. My goal was to take the drug money I was making and invest it into the music business like I had seen so many others before my time do. Like Master P's no limit and Baby and Slim the owners of Cash Money records. They had made it successfully out of the drug game by investing their money into something positive. What I didn't know is that it was a slim chance of that happening inside our communities before getting caught and going to prison for the rest of your life or being killed.

You see most of the time its only two ways selling drugs end, you either going to be dead or in jail. You're either going to do right, or you're going to do wrong, because the two don't mix. The bible says that you're going to either serve God or the devil, but you can't serve both. I purchased studio time and started working on my first album "Ball Till They Pour Da Dirt". The first single off that album was called "Ball Till They Pour Da Dirt". I took on the name Jamerican Prince as my stage name because my dad was Jamaican and my mom was an American. Plus I felt like a Prince because all of the money I was making. After recording my first single I orchestrated a music video to it.

My community came out and supported me on it. After shooting my music video I pressed up VHS copies and sold them out my trunk throughout my neighborhood, state and surrounding states for $10 a copy. I made $1,000 off my first run. Once the whole album was finished I began to sell copies of the album out my trunk and set up consignment at different urban clothing and music stores to sell my album for a small profit. My album sold for $10 a copy. I put together a street team of youth to travel with me. It was 6 of us. I would tell my team to sell the albums for $10 a copy.

I would tell them they would make $5 off each copy they sold. I would teach them the sales pitch and how to ask for support while letting customers know I had major artists featuring on this album. At that time I was recording songs with Pastor Troy and Smoke from "Field Mob. I began traveling throughout the south performing my music and opening up for major artist from Lil Wayne, Field Mob, Pastor Troy, Kia, No Good, Juvenile, JT Money and many more artist.

I was living a dream, all the while I was a king pin in my city moving large amounts of cocaine a week bringing in sometimes $15,000 a day. The streets had me trapped. What is it to gain the world and lose your soul? This was truly the trick of the enemy. While I was performing, partying and selling drugs my life that I thought was skyrocketing was really going in a downward spiral.

What did you learn? How will you implement?

_____

_____

_____

_____

_____

_____

_____

_____

_____

_____

_____

_____

_____

_____

_____

_____

_____

_____

_____

_____

_____

_____

Chapter 20

Shady Business

I had a cousin by the name of Lil L. Lil L was 5'10, light skinned, with light brown eyes. Lil L had just graduated from high school. Lil L had seen the money Biggie and I was making on the streets selling drugs and all the nice things we had that came with it. Lil L chose not to go to college. Instead he chose to follow after Biggie and I getting money in the streets. I hooked Lil L up with some of my clientele to get him started. Lil had a passion for the entertainment business just like I did.

Lil L believed in my music career and would travel with me promoting my music career. Lil L would be apart of my music videos and commercials that I would advertise on television when I first started. Lil L and I invested $4500 to have some promotions done that was stolen from us. The guy I was working with had written up some fake contracts and was using them to take people money.

We had fallen victim after Lil L and I went half on the $4500. We did everything we could to track the guy down, but never found him. We had to charge that $4500 to the game. Nevertheless, that didn't stop us from pursuing my music career. We understood from there that the music business was a shady game and that it didn't play fair. The music business was just like being in the streets. Lil and I would spend a lot of time together.

What did you learn? How will you implement?

Chapter 21

Rocky

In the beginning of my music career right after I finished my "Ball Till They Pour Da Dirt" music video I had fallen head over hills for a woman name Rocky who was several years older than me. Rocky had a body like Jessica Rabbit with all the curves, brown skinned, about 5'5, 140 pounds, very pretty, brown eyes and wore her hair short like Halle Berry. Her child father whom she had been with had gone to federal prison. One day I pulled up to the restaurant that she owned with her child father and started a conversation with her.

"Hey beautiful, how are you?" I asked "Hey, I'm good, how are you?" she replied "I'm great, may I ask your name?", I asked "Sure, I'm Rocky", she said. Well do you know who I am?" I asked "Yes I do, you're Jamerican Prince", she said. "That's correct", I said very surprised that she knew who I was. "You use to always be checking me out by Spains bar when I lived with my grandma", she added. Yes you are definitely correct. "I've been checking you out for a while, but just was waiting until the right time to say something", I said.

"O Ok, you should've been said something", she said. "Yea you right, do you mind if I have your number, so I can follow up with dinner and possibly get to know each other a little more," I suggested. "Sure", she said. After several minutes of conversation I was able to get a phone number and a date out. Rocky and I had fallen in love with each other. I always wanted Rocky by my side and hated to be away from her. Rocky wasn't an ordinary woman, there was something special about her.

She was very intelligent and smart. Rocky was a true hustler; Rocky helped me to take the drug game to another level. Rocky had a friend, who had a cousin that was very strong in the game. Rocky and her friend would get quarter keys from her friend's cousin and then she would front it to Biggie. After numerous times of fronting ounces from the quarter key to biggie, she then let me in on the deal. I never knew why she didn't let me in on the deal earlier, but I was glad to be in.

Rocky introduced me to more cocaine then I had ever seen in my life. Rocky started off feeding Biggie and I quarter keys. We would sell them so fast that she had to up her game and bring a larger quantity to keep from going back so fast. So one day I made a suggestion to biggie that we needed to sell powder instead of cooking the powder into crack cocaine, which we had become master chefs at doing.

I told him we could make a faster flip since all the drug dealers are cooking their own crack. We can just be the supplier since we are getting it so cheap. By that time Rocky had started to get half keys of cocaine from her supplier for us to sell. Once we had done saved up enough to buy our own half of keys of cocaine, we stopped fronting from Rocky. Rocky had done made so much money off of us, she had already saved up. Soon Biggie and I was purchasing Keys of cocaine supplying half of Melbourne if not all. We were on super strong. The more money we made the more flashier we were and the more money I made, the more I invested into my record label I had then started.

What did you learn? How will you implement?

_____

_____

_____

_____

_____

_____

_____

_____

_____

_____

_____

_____

_____

_____

_____

_____

_____

_____

_____

_____

Chapter 22

The Good Life

Biggie and I would compare how much money we were making each day. Biggie and I was real close and was inseparable. Once our lease was up in Woodfield apartments, we then relocated to a 3-bedroom house out in Palm Bay, Fl that we were renting. Rocky was always at our apartment in Woodfield, so when we moved she ended up moving in with Biggie, Biggie's girlfriend Mitch, and I. After a few months living in Palm Bay my younger brother Kenneth moved in. Our house driveway was full of nice cars Biggie and I had put a lot of money into.

If I would have known what I know now, I would have never thrown my money away like that. I would have took that money and invested in property and rental property, or something I knew would bring me a return in investment. Being so one-track minded, I never looked to invest into anything but music. Our house definitely looked like a home for drug dealers occupied with all the nice cars and no one going to work each day. I mean we could have been superstars in the entertainment business but the chances of that was slim coming from our city.

As Biggie and I rose to the top of the dope game I started feeling like Biggie had started hating on me and competing with me, because of the things he would do and say to other people about me. Biggie would make comments about Rocky that I didn't agree with. Then he would make comments to other people about me. Rocky was the finest chick in town, so I always caught hate behind that because the guys that wanted her couldn't get her.

Rocky always loved my drive and motivation. She always knew it was something special about me. That was different from the rest. Rocky had started feeling very uncomfortable being in the house because of the people Biggie was trusting to come over. Biggie thought everyone was his friend. Biggie had a kind heart even though he had his ways. Rocky would talk to Mitch and was very uncomfortable with Mitch being in the house alone at night also.

Rocky had convinced me to leave the dope game and come with her to Atlanta to start a new life. I was very hesitate because I was so strong in the game. I couldn't see myself doing anything else but I myself had started feeling the hate, and the danger of being a big time drug dealer. Everyone around us was being robbed, including my older and younger brother Kenneth and Biggies brother Half-pint.

What made it so bad was, it was the same guys doing the robbing and no one out of our family wanted to retaliate. My family was very family orientated and didn't play about one another but the money had caused some of us to let our guards down.

After being convinced by Rocky to let everything go and come with her to Atlanta, I decided to try and find a place to live to start a new life. I talked with Biggie and told him Rocky and my plan.

Biggie didn't really agree with it but he knew I was my own man and I was going to make this decision by myself. After a couple of days, Rocky and I packed a few clothes and headed to Atlanta. After being in Atlanta a few days I received a phone call on my cell. "Hello", I answered. "May I speak with Kent Osbourne", said the guy on the other end.

"Yea this is him, may I ask who's calling", I asked. "Yea this is officer John with the Palm Bay Police Department, we need for you to come in for questioning", said the officer. "Why what's going on", I said as my heart started to pound because I was afraid. "Biggie and Mitch were shot in a home invasion, one person is deceased and the other is fighting for their life", said the officer.

"What", I yelled! "I'm on my way", I said as I hung up the phone. "Baby what's going on", said Rocky. "Somebody broke in the house and shot Biggie and Mitch, I'm going to kill them niggas", I screamed as I punched a hole in the wall. "Pack up your things and let's go", I yelled. Rocky and I packed our things and headed back to Florida trying to figure out who in the world could have done this.

What did you learn? How will you implement?

Chapter 23

Consequences

After finding out Biggie was shot twice in the head and Mitch was shot multiple times before being shot in the head point blank range while she was several months pregnant and died from her wounds, I was devasted. I couldn't think of nothing else but finding the people who did this and seeking revenge. It didn't take long for my family to figure out the killers who were the same guys that had robbed Biggie's brother Half-Pint and my two brothers.

While Biggie was still alive fighting for his life in the hospital, several family members and I had gathered together at one of my older cousins house. We put a plan together to execute every one of their family members that were gathered at a family outing that was taking place. We all jogged in all black, masked up through a neighborhood known as Booker Heights where I spent most of my teenage and adult years.

Once we had arrived, we posted up on the side of the house and prepared for the massacre. See, we had just rode by this house earlier and seen several of the killers family members outside barbequing and having a magnificent time. Little did they know that was fixing to be cut short. As I stood there with my family waiting for the right moment to strike all I could think about was Biggie laying up in that hospital bed fighting for his life and Mitch and my unborn baby cousin shot to death execution style.

At this moment I wasn't worried about the consequences and repercussions of carrying out a gruesome attack as this. I just felt anger and rage as I stood there with sweat absorbing into my mask, not afraid, but anxious to carry out the attack. I was ready to do whatever it took to revenge Biggie and the death of Mitch and my unborn cousin. Since we couldn't find the killers who had been running and hiding out from us, we just decided to take away their loved ones for revenge. Then maybe that would bring them cowards out.

Once we prepared ourselves, we ran from around the corner with our weapons drawn. As we got ready to fire our weapons we noticed every family member that was out there earlier wasn't there anymore. It was like God had warned them that something terrible was about to happen and had told them to leave. We turned around and jogged back to my cousin house where we took shelter.

After not completing the mission I thought about it. What if we had completed the mission and the families of the killers were ambushed and killed. There would have been a motive.

What if the police caught just one of my family members who participated and that family member told on all the rest of us to get him a lighter sentence. I wouldn't be here telling this story today. Everything happens for a reason. I look at it as a blessing that the killers family members weren't outside because there wouldn't be a Kent Osbourne telling this story today.

What did you learn? How will you implement?

_____

_____

_____

_____

_____

_____

_____

_____

_____

_____

_____

_____

_____

_____

_____

_____

_____

_____

_____

_____

_____

_____

_____

Chapter 24

Black Lives Matter

A few months had passed. Biggie and Mitch attackers had turned themselves in within the first couple of months of their warrants. Biggie had survived the attack. Biggie was able to make a statement and describe the two killers, who he knew very well and had done drug transactions with in the past. One of the killers had been an employee with Mitch at a local restaurant where she worked.

There was nowhere they could go and be safe without the cops, my family and me looking for them. The cops had marked them armed and dangerous. We had them marked as dead men if we got to them first. Rocky and I had gone back to Atlanta to carry out our plan to move and start a new life.

While Rocky and I was in Atlanta, I was pulled over for a traffic citation and taken to jail for a warrant out of Polk County, Fl. Polk County had violated my probation that they had put me on a couple years back. I sat in the Polk County Jail a month before I was released on house arrest. I was able to have my house arrest transferred back to my hometown in Melbourne, Fl. Rocky and I had rented a two-bedroom apartment, it was there I did my house arrest.

Rocky had 3 kids along the ages of 7-12, which she didn't tell me about until later in our relationship. Rocky 3 kids moved in with Rocky and I. After Biggie got out the hospital, him and Half-Pint stopped by to see me. I was glad Biggie had stopped by. It was awesome to see Biggie alive. I just hated to see Biggie with a tube placed in his throat that he used to breath. Never the less it didn't stop Biggie from smoking a blunt because when him and Half-Pint came over they were smoking. I didn't smoke with Biggie and Half-Pint because I was on house arrest.

What did you learn? How will you implement?

Chapter 25

Baby Daddy Drama

One day Rocky baby father called the house from the Federal Institution. He asked to speak to his children, which he called all of them because he helped raise them before going to Federal Prison. Once he was done talking to them he wanted to talk with Rocky. I got so angry and took the phone. "What's up partner, you said you wanted to talk to the kids not Rocky", I said. "Well she has my kids so I need to talk to her", he said. "What about the kids, there isn't anything you can do for them in there, plus only one is yours", I said.

"If I want to talk to my kids mother I will", he said. "No you will not, you better not call here anymore, this is my woman", I yelled! "You need to be trying not to drop that soap punk", I yelled again! After going back and fourth I hung up the phone and told Rocky that she better not allow him to call her.

What did you learn? How will you implement?

_____

_____

_____

_____

_____

_____

_____

_____

_____

_____

_____

_____

_____

_____

_____

_____

_____

_____

_____

_____

_____

Chapter 26

Hellraiser

I had fallen off. Rocky and I didn't have the cocaine connection we had before we decided to let the game go and head to Atlanta. I had to start from the bottom again. Rocky still had a few thousand dollars she held on to while we were in Atlanta. I had spent all my money into getting music and TV's put into my box Chevy before leaving to go to Atlanta. Only reason I decided to put all my money into my car, which was a total of $12,000 which I had left was because Rocky had told me to spend it all and she would have my back but boy was that a mistake!

I had to depend on her and whenever we would argue Rocky would tell me how broke I was and curse me out. Biggie had started feeling like Rocky had something to do with him getting shot, but I knew that wasn't true because Rocky loved Biggie and looked out for him. Rocky was my girl and she wouldn't do anything like that to someone I loved. If she was going to do that, she might as well had done it to me. Rocky had gotten into real estate. Rocky applied for jobs and started to work a nine to five real job.

Rocky had also started to attend church. Rocky would always try to get me to come to church with her, I would never want to go. I was into the street life and didn't want to hear nothing about God. Rocky had one foot in the church and one foot out. She would tell me about God then she would be gambling and cursing me out the next minute. Rocky and my relationship had started to decline. Rocky had shown me a picture from spring break of a man penis that stretched down his leg. She insisted that her and her girlfriends thought it was funny and laughed about it and that she figured she could share it with me.

I didn't look at it as a laughing matter, I was furious. I instantly accused her of cheating on me while at spring break. A year later I cheated on Rocky. Rocky knew I had been with somebody but she couldn't prove it. Rocky would bring it up all the time for me to admit I had been with somebody and that if I would admit it we could move on. I felt Rocky had started to deal with other people also because she knew what I had done. A year later I ended up admitting to Rocky that I had cheated. Rocky and I had established a relationship where we would break up and get back together. We had started seeing other people. I had by then moved in my own apartment.

One day I was talking to Rocky on the phone, I still loved Rocky no matter what we went through. She had allowed her baby father which I didn't get along with at the time to come over and do some handy man work and boy was I furious. "What you got that nigga over your house?" I yelled! "Yea he fixing my walls, what it matter to you, this is my house I can have who I want in here", yelled Rocky! "O yea, I'm on my way", I yelled! I ran out the house and got in my car and fled over to Rocky house, which was in the neighboring city from where I lived. As I pulled up in the driveway I noticed a truck in the yard, I jumped out my car and slammed the door.

I walked up to the door and opened it without knocking and went in. When I walked in I seen her baby father inside the house, boy was I angry. He was a six feet 170 pound man with a slim build, short haircut, dark skinned man. He was much older than I was. I went from zero to 100 real quick. "You got this pussy nigger up in your house", I screamed! "Get out my house", screamed Rocky! "I'm not going nowhere, you got this fuck nigger in here, tell him to leave", I yelled! As I kept screaming and calling him out his name taking his manhood, he got upset and started to scream back.

"Hey man you're not going to be disrespecting me like that, my kids live here and I'm going to do whatever necessary to make sure they are straight", he yelled! "No you are not fuck nigger, I already told you this is my woman and I don't want you around her", I screamed! He started walking out the door to leave; as he was walking out the door he started selling out. I started following him out the door yelling back. During this time, Rocky's daughter who was there with her two other brothers grabbed a knife to defend her stepfather and mother. She started coming towards me.

"O you're going to stab me", I yelled! "I'm not afraid of no knife", I screamed! Rocky older son Terrell grabbed the knife out his sister hand. As Rocky baby daddy made his way out the front door I followed him cursing and screaming. As Rocky baby daddy made his way to his truck, he was yelling back at me. I continued to walk toward him as he was placing his tools in his truck and bam! I stuck him with a blow to the face and we started fighting. "What's up pussy nigger", I yelled as I was throwing blow after blow using everything I had learned when I was boxing at University Boxing Club and Palm Bay Boxing Association.

I was trained and ready for war and to battle. Fighting wasn't anything I wasn't use to. I made sure he didn't land any blows because I was throwing mine fast and consistent leaving no time for him to land anything. I already had it in for him because how he was selling me out on the phone years earlier when he called our home and I had told him to not drop the soap which was a phrase used to prisoners.

After a couple of my blows landed to his head we locked up and started to wrestle. With both of us breathing hard I managed to get behind him and put him in a choke hole. As I put my arm around his neck he managed to bite a plug out my arm. I started to hit him harder with blows to the head to get him to release the bite.

"O your going to bite me like a bitch fuck nigger", I yelled! He wasn't saying anything; he was just fighting for his life. Shortly after the fight Rocky's older son came out to break up the fight. "Come on man ya'll stop this", he said as he made his way between us. We both was exhausted so it was easy for Rocky's son to break up the fight.

As he started walking away from the fight I was still angry and wanted to continue the fight. "Where you going pussy nigger come back and fight like a man", I yelled walking behind him. He jumped in his truck and sped off. As he took off I picked up a brick and slung it at his truck. It hit the side of his truck and put a huge dent in the side.

He continued on down the road. By that time Rocky had called the police, I jumped in my truck and sped off down the road where I was stopped, confronted and searched by the Palm Bay Police Department. Rocky had reported to them that I had a gun on me. After several minutes I was released.

What did you learn? How will you implement?

_____

_____

_____

_____

_____

_____

_____

_____

_____

_____

_____

_____

_____

_____

_____

_____

_____

_____

_____

_____

_____

_____

_____

_____

_____

_____

_____

_____

_____

_____

_____

_____

_____

_____

_____

_____

_____

_____

_____

_____

_____

_____

_____

_____

_____

_____

Chapter 27

Ghetto Got Me Trap

One night lil L and I was riding. I had then popped an ecstasy pill and was feeling real good! We had a bottle of Hennessy we was drinking on and smoking a blunt. We pulled up to the club and it was thick outside. A lot of people from the neighborhood hung out there on the weekends. As we pulled up there were cops standing outside that I didn't see. I parked right in front of the club and jumped out with a blunt in my mouth puffing away, with a cup of Hennessy in my hand. The cop watched me as I got out with the blunt in my mouth and the cup in my hand.

As I walked over to talk to a cousin of mine that was there, I was met halfway by the officer that told me to put the blunt out and put my hands behind my back. I was so high off the ecstasy pills and weed, every time the officer tried to put my hands behind my back I kept slipping my hand away from the cuffs. I had drugs in my pocket. I looked over at lil L and asked him to help me as the cops tussled with me to get my hands behind my back. There was nothing lil L could do to help me out with this situation when it came to the cops arresting me, I was just drunk and high and wasn't in my right mind to ask lil L to help me fight these cops and escape.

The cops finally got my hand behind my back as I stopped resisting. They searched my car and didn't find anything. When they searched me they found a few ecstasy pills that I had on me. They put me in the police car, I gave lil L the keys and off to jail I went. Jail wasn't anything I wasn't use to because I had been in and out most of my life. I bonded out a few days after. After being released I hooked up with a partner of mine out of Orlando, Florida who was into pimping women using an escort service.

He showed me the ropes, and I got into the pimping business. I would drive the women to the hotels and wait for them to go in and bring me the money out. Once I had learned the ropes a little, I found me a girl of my own to pimp and went into business. In the pimping business you had to make the woman fall in love with you by having sex with her continuously, all the time, so that she would do anything for you. You basically messed with her head.

My partner had told me it was better to use a white girl but I had a black girlfriend that was down with it that I used to pimp. She was use to the game because she had done it before. She got real rebellious and didn't want to give me her money after she performed the services. Pimping didn't last long for me, I wasn't as good at it as my partner was so I got out of it. When I went back home to take a urine test that I was required to take while on probation for a charge I caught earlier, I violated and was reinstated.

What did you learn? How will you implement?

_____

_____

_____

_____

_____

_____

_____

_____

_____

_____

_____

_____

_____

_____

_____

_____

_____

_____

_____

_____

Chapter 28

Game Over

Even after Rocky had called the cops on me for coming over to her house and jumping on her baby father, I still loved Rocky. She still loved me. Our relationship was bitter sweet. Even though we would date other people we still would always come back to each other and make some great break up to make up love. Now I had moved into a boarding house with several other roommates. A boarding house is 1 house shared by other tenants that occupy the same space. It was 4 of us that lived inside this boarding house.

I occupied the attic that was turned into a room. I didn't know that one of the tenants that was there had been selling drugs out the house. I was selling drugs but not out the house. I would go meet my customers down the street or at their house. One night I heard a loud bang on the door. I immediately jumped up and jumped out the attic window onto the ground which was two floors up.

As I landed on the ground I took off running down the street with just my boxers on. When I got to the end of the road I saw a cop car. I ran up to the cop car and told the officer what had just happened, that someone broke into my house and I jumped out the window and ran. The cop couldn't believe what he was hearing. "You mean to tell me you jumped out the attic window", asked the cop. "Yes I was afraid", I said breathing hard from the entire running I just did. "Get in and show me where you just ran from", said the cop.

I got in the back of the police car as we headed down the street to the boarding house. As we got closer I seen the cops bring the tenants out that lived there with me. I knew right then that it was a bust. I figured I would be ok because I hadn't sold any drugs out the house and that they wouldn't be able to go in my room and search for nothing being that all the tenants occupied their own space, but little did I know.

"Now show me where you jumped from", said the cop. "From up there", I said as I pointed to the top of the house at the attic. "You mean to tell me you jumped from up there", said the cop in amazement. "Yes", I said. "Stay right here", said the cop. The cop got out and went and talked with the other cops. When the cop came back, he told me what was going on, that the house was being busted for cocaine and that they found a pill bottle full of crack and some weed in my room.

Then the cop took me out the police car and put me in hand cuffs and had me to stand beside the other tenants who were also in handcuffs at the time. When everything was over, the actual guy who had sold the drugs out the house and I was sent to jail. The other two tenants were set free, because they didn't find anything on them or in their rooms. I had violated my probation that I was placed on from a charge two years ago with a new charge now. I was placed in the county jail with no bond as I awaited sentencing and was sent to prison for the second time in my life for 20 months.

What did you learn? How will you implement?

Chapter 29

Seek Ye First (Mathew 6:33)

As I'm riding on the blue bird, all I could think about was how I really messed up this time. I had just signed a distribution deal with Matordor/Universal to release several albums off of my Rapid Fire Records 2 label. I had felt like I let everybody down. It was a long sad ride for me and several disappointing weeks leading up to me being placed in a permanent facility.

I had been down this road before but it was something very different about this time. I never imagined in a million years I would be back in this place, especially at this time in my life. I was a superstar in my region. I had put out several cd's and had songs with top recording artist. I had opened up on stage for the hottest artist out. I couldn't believe I was locked back up again. As we pulled up into the security checkpoint fence and entered the facility of Liberty Correctional Institution. I went through the same procedures for intake as the first time going to prison.

After the intake process I was sent to Liberty Correctional Institution work camp. Once at the work camp I started to follow the usual routine of my incarcerations. Get up in the mornings after cleaning up and head outside to the weight pile to workout. The officers would send us outside every morning anyway for cleanup for several hours. I would work out and spend my time reading books. I would read a lot of James Patterson books. One day on the rec yard I met a guy by the name of Mathew.

Mathew was a black male about 5'7 with short black hair and brown eyes. Mathew had 16 gold teeth in his mouth just like I did, 8 to the top and 8 at the bottom, with tattoos on his arm. Mathew and I had become good friends after seeing me rapping outside on the rec yard. I shared with Mathew how I was this great gangster rap artist and all of the success I had achieved, which really wasn't true success because of the fact I kept ending up behind bars while pursuing this so called fame and success.

Mathew shared with me some information that would go on to change my life forever. He told me about a man named Jesus, which I knew about. My mom brought me up knowing about this man. Plus my aunt kept us in Church where they taught about Jesus. Rocky would also try to get me to come to church whenever she would go.

"Kent if you want to be successful you need to give your life to God and anything that you want out of life it could happen for you bruh, come to church with me", said Mathew. "Yea, you mean to tell me God will be able to make me successful in my music and keep me out of prison", I asked? "Yes bruh, he will do it for you, all you have to do is come to church with me bruh", said Mathew. Now that I look back at what Mathew was telling me was the scripture in the bible Mathew 6:33 that says; Seek ye first the kingdom of God and his righteousness and all these things shall be added unto you. "Ok I'll come", I told Mathew.

They had church almost every night in prison as it was needed. As I started to go to church with Mathew almost every night of the week, which was held in a portable that was on the prison campus, I started to learn more about Christ love and how he had died on the cross for my sins. (John 3:16) For God so loved the world that he gave his only begotten son, that whoever believes in him shall not perish but have eternal life. I started to learn that no matter what you have done in life, God could still use you.

I learned about sin and what it was. I learned that sinned led to death but I could be forgiven for it. (1 John 1:9) If we confess our sins, he is faithful and just to forgive us our sins and to cleanse us from all unrighteousness. After being educated on Christ fully after several weeks of going to church I gave my life to Christ. (Romans 10:9-10) If you declare with your mouth, "Jesus is Lord," and believe in your heart that God raised him from the dead you will be saved.

What did you learn? How will you implement?

Chapter 30

Born Again (John 3:4)

I stopped reading all the James Patterson books I was reading and started reading the bible only. The more I read and went to church I started to build a personal relationship with Christ. (Romans 10:17) Faith cometh by hearing and hearing by the word of God. I would continue to write music during my incarceration because of the passion I had for it, plus I had a release date so I knew it wasn't over for me as for my musical dream. I would continue to write the music I was writing that promoted violence, sex and guns, then on the other hand I would write music geared towards God.

As my personal relationship started to grow more in Christ, I learned his commandments and what he required. I didn't want to do anything to hurt God. (John 14:15) "If you love me, keep my commands". You see when you fall in love with Christ it's like falling in love with a women, you will do anything you can to keep from hurting that person and you will do your best to make them happy because you love them so much.

I stopped writing all that negative music I was writing and started to devote all my energy and time into writing spiritual music. I started to apply the knowledge I was getting out the bible to my life, that's when my life begun to change. When I would go to church I was able to perform my written material to instrumentals that was brought in through the prison chaplains. One day there were certain prophets that was there that seen me perform. "Kent we see you travelling all over the world reaching kids through your music", said the prophets.

By hearing this it encouraged me to go even further with the plans God had for my life. (Jeremiah 29:11) "For I know the plans I have for you, declares the Lord, plans to prosper you and not to harm you, plans to give you hope and a future". After 8 months at Liberty Correctional Institute I was sent to work release for the remaining 8 months of my sentence.

While in work release I was able to go to an outside church in the community off DOC facilities. I became a member of Promiseland Church. Promiseland had ministers of the church who would come to the work release and pick up inmates and drop them back off after church. At Promiseland I found a new home and a new father in Christ by the name of Pastor Mcclure. Pastor Mcclure allowed me to get on stage and share my testimony and also allowed me to perform. Promiseland was a mixed church of different race.

When I would get on stage and share my testimony lots of the congregation fell in love with my testimony.

I started to blossom as I became a regular gospel musician at Promiseland ministering through music on Sundays. After 8 months incarceration in work release I was released back to society. I kept working at Liberty Recycling in Rockledge, Fl., which was the job I worked while in work release. I stayed a member of Promiseland and attended every week. I started to go to different churches to ask if I could share my testimony and perform.

As I would perform at different churches there would always be someone from another church that wanted me to come share my testimony and perform at their church. Word of mouth got out and I was performing at every church in my community. Nine years later in 2018 I am the owner of K.O Trucking LLC which grosses 6 figures a year, Generation Changers International LLC a Record Label I started to executive produce, market and promote all my music.

I also have a nonprofit organization Prison To Power in which I am the founder and President. I've also branched out into motivational speaking and acting. I'm also an author now! I'm a true example that God can use anybody. I don't care where you are in life or what you been through, God can still use you! Like I always say, which is one of my favorite quotes,

"If I can do it, you can do it"! "If God did it for me he'll do it for you"! To God be the glory! The End.

After hearing my story and you feel stuck in life and have experienced some of the same things I've experienced, or are going through some of these same things if not all at this moment and you want your life to change for the better to experience all that God has for you and to bring out the greatness inside of you so that you can live a prosperous, fulfilling, and successful life, I want you to repeat after me. "Lord I am a sinner. I believe you died on the cross for my sins and arose from the dead. Jesus I believe you are the son of God". If you said this prayer after me you are saved. What I need you to do now is find you a bible teaching church to join so you can learn God's commandments and the plans he has for your life. Be blessed, I'm excited about your future!

What did you learn? How will you implement?

_____

_____

_____

_____

_____

_____

_____

_____

_____

_____

_____

_____

_____

_____

_____

_____

_____

_____

_____

_____

_____

ABOUT AUTHOR

Kent Osbourne is a go getter and a relentless entrepreneur. Kent Osbourne is the owner of three businesses. K.O Trucking LLC, Generation Changers International LLC (Record Label), and Prison To Power non-Profit. Kent is also a motivational speaker that reaches back into the communities motivating and empowering others that they to can be great and go from prison to power visiting prisons, detention centers, ect. Kent Osbourne days haven't always been so bright. He's had his dark days. Kent Osbourne faced challenges in life that would have made most throw in the towel. Kent has overcame all obstacles, trials and tribulations, and road blocks life has thrown at him to become the man he is today. In just a few years Kent went from Prison to Power. Kent is an inspiration to be enjoyed.

STAY CONNECTED TO KENT OSBOURNE

From motivational videos to powerful music and more, www.KentOsbourne.com is full of inspiration that will give you the encouragement and confidence to live your best life.

HIRE KENT OSBOURNE TODAY

Need a Lifestyle Coach, Mentor, Motivational Speaker or Singer? Visit www.KentOsbourne.com for more information.

22580381R00087

Made in the USA
Columbia, SC
02 August 2018